Pet Owner's Guide to the
BOXER

Andrew H. Brace

RINGPRESS

RINGPRESS

Published by Ringpress Books Limited,
PO Box 8, Lydney, Gloucestershire
GL15 6YD, United Kingdom.

First Published 1996
© 1996 Ringpress Books Limited.
All rights reserved

ISBN 1 86054 065 1

Printed and bound in Hong Kong

Contents

About the author

Andrew H. Brace is one of the UK's leading all-rounder judges, approved to award Kennel Club Challenge Certificates in some fifty breeds. In addition, he has been approved to judge Best in Show at Championship level, as well as the Working, Utility, Toy and Hound Groups.

A prolific writer on canine matters, Andrew was Editor and Publisher of *Dogs Monthly*, a glossy, specialist magazine with a readership in forty different countries. He also founded, edited and published *Boxer Quarterly*, which was considered a milestone in British breed publications, proving immensely popular with Boxer owners internationally. For many years, Andrew has written a weekly column in the British paper *Dog World*, as well as making monthly contributions to the USA's *Dog News*, Australia's *Ozdog*, and more recently for *Dogs In Canada*. In 1994 Ringpress Books published *The Essential Guide to Judging Dogs*, Andrew's first title, which has been internationally acclaimed.

As a breeder and exhibitor, Andrew is best known for his Beagles, the most famous to carry his Tragband affix being Ch. Too Darn Hot For Tragband, who remains the top winning Beagle of all time in the UK.

> *This book is dedicated to the memory of Bruce, my first-ever pedigree dog, a Boxer. Although Bruce never saw the inside of a show ring, he kindled in me a fascination and passion for the world of show dogs and dog shows which has never waned. My best friend through those difficult teenage years, Bruce died tragically young, but he will always have a special place in my heart.*
>
> **A.H.B.**

Photography: Carol Ann Johnson

Facing page picture: Diane Pearce

Chapter One

HISTORY OF THE BOXER

THE BOXER LEGEND

The modern Boxer owes its early origins to the combination of a German hunting and baiting breed, known as the Bullenbeisser, and the primitive English Bulldog. However, a much more charming account comes in the shape of a legend which has been passed down among German peasants for generations. This is quoted in Herr Philip Stockmann's book on the breed:

"In the beginning was the Creation, and on the Sixth Day, after the world and the heavens were made, God created the animals to inhabit it, in every possible variety for every possible purpose; and he created Man to have dominion over the animals. But so that Man should not be alone among the animals, He made one animal to be Man's friend – the dog. And He made the dogs in many different forms so that every man could choose his favourite companion – large and small, tall and short, brown, black, white, spotted and striped, shaggy and smooth. And God saw that they were good. So good that He said 'I will make one dog who is supreme, one above all other dogs, who shall have beauty, strength, speed and courage blended subtly with loyalty, nobility, watchfulness and friendliness.'

"So He took soft clay and from it fashioned the ideal dog, in the shape of a Boxer, except that, like other dogs, he had a long, sensitive, elegant nose, the very acme of noses. As He put it aside to harden, God was pleased, and said 'Truly this is the perfect dog.'

"Now although the Boxer had not hardened, he was in all other respects complete, and he heard what God said about him, which made him very proud. Therefore, as he went his way, he said to the other dogs 'I am the perfect dog, because I heard God say so. Look at me and you must admit that I am a better dog than you.' The little dogs agreed at once; the medium dogs were not so sure but were not prepared to dispute the point; but the large dogs were decidedly annoyed, for were they not bigger and stronger than the Boxer? They said as much, taunting the Boxer for his size, until in a rage the Boxer hurled himself upon the largest.

"But alas! He had forgotten that he was still soft, and his beautiful nose, the symmetrical perfection of all noses, was squashed flat, his smooth face was all wrinkled, and when he saw this he was very worried.

"Then God, who had seen all that had taken place, smiled, and said 'Because you are my favourite, you shall have only the punishment you have made for yourself. For all time you must wear your face as you have made it this day.'

"That this is true cannot be doubted, because to this day, the Boxer meets all small dogs with courtesy and will not harm them; but he has not forgiven the large dogs, and if provoked, will still hurl himself upon them in rage."

Anyone who has shared their life with a Boxer will fully understand that he was God's favourite, and the many endearing attributes of the breed mentioned in this delightful piece of folklore persist to this day.

NAMING THE BREED

Legend apart, there have been several theories put forward as to the origin of the breed's name. Some sources claim that, as the medium-sized Bullenbeisser was also known as the 'Boxl', this term became bastardised into 'Boxer'. A less credible explanation is that, due to the Boxer's readiness to play-fight with his paws while standing on his hindlegs, he was given the pugilist's label.

Though the word 'boxer' translates identically into German, it seems unlikely that such a proud nation would give one of its greatest creations such an obviously anglicised name!

THE FIRST BOXERS

Towards the end of the nineteenth century, a resident of Munich, named Georg Alt, produced a bitch who was called Alt's Schecken. Previously Alt had mated Flora, a brindle-coloured bitch of medium Bullenbeisser type, which he had imported from France, to a local dog of unknown ancestry, but known simply as 'Boxer'. The union resulted in a fawn and white male, this dog taking his owner's name to become simply 'Lechner's Boxer.' He was in turn mated back to his own dam, Flora, and one of their offspring was Schecken.

Schecken was later mated to an English Bulldog called Tom who produced the historically significant dog called Flocki. Flocki earned his place in Boxer history by becoming the very first Boxer to enter the German Stud Book. He did so by winning at a Munich show for St Bernards – the first event to schedule a class for Boxers. While Flocki may have been Number One in the Stud Book, his sister, Ch. Blanka von Angertor, a white bitch, was to be of greater influence. When Blanka was mated to Piccolo von Angertor (a grandson of Lechner's Boxer, Blanka's grandsire), she produced a predominantly white bitch called Meta von der Passage, who is still considered to be the mother of the breed.

Early photographs of Meta show her to be rather long and weak-backed, less than straight-fronted, and quite down-faced. Yet through her progeny she provided a foundation for the future of the breed to which, now, she bears little resemblance.

THE FIRST BREED CLUB

In 1896 the German Boxer Club was formed and in March of that year the Club held its first show, which attracted twenty entries for the judge, Elard Konig. We are told that several of the entered dogs were white, or white with patches of either brindle or fawn, while others were black. It is interesting to discover that many of the early specimens were white, a colour which was later to be outlawed by the Breed Standard because of the risk of deafness in white dogs. However, white-coloured Boxers still crop up regularly in present-day litters.

Following its first show, the parent club set about establishing a Standard for the Boxer. It is claimed that this task took six years, and the finalised Breed Standard for the Boxer was eventually adopted in January 1902.

In the USA, the breed has cropped ears.

Photo: Teoh Eng Hong.

Many of the first Boxers were white or white with patches of fawn or brindle. Today, it is the classic white markings which are sought-after, and all-white Boxers are never exhibited in the show ring.

According to legend, the Boxer was chosen as God's favourite – there is no doubt that the breed's impressive appearance and charming character has gained it universal popularity.

Diane Pearce.

BREED PIONEERS

Some seven years later, in 1909, a young German lady who was studying art and sculpture in Munich, met up with a young man who proved to be a Boxer owner. The lady, named Friederun, first became enchanted with the Boxer breed when she saw a photograph in a book of dog breeds given to her for Christmas by her brother. She longed for a Boxer from that day forward and, having discovered that Philip Stockmann owned such a dog, she encouraged their friendship and subsequently they were married. Herr Stockmann's dog, Pluto, became his bride's most devoted companion and awakened in her the desire to learn more about the breed.

Frau Stockmann's contribution to the breed can never be over-estimated. In subsequent years she and her husband established the legendary Kennel von Dom, which produced some of the most famous and significant dogs in the breed's history. In her book, *My Life With Boxers*, she relates her most fascinating life story, and tells of the hardship and the heartaches she faced – and the moments of joy – while struggling to keep her kennel alive through the war years. This book is now very much a collector's item, and those Boxer owners who are fortunate enough to own a copy will never let it out of their possession. It is one of the most moving books I have ever read, and Frau Stockmann's own illustrations are a delight.

Friederun Stockmann was a gifted sculptress, and her pieces are very much treasured by connoisseurs. Bearing in mind the famous Boxer legend, it somehow seems as if fate decreed that such a talented artist should adopt, pioneer and advance God's most perfect dog.

In later years, the German, Dutch, British and American Boxers may have evolved along slightly different lines, but there can be no disputing the fact that all owe their foundation to Frau Stockmann and her von Doms. The influence of key dogs such as Sigurd von Dom, his son Zorn von Dom, and grandsons Utz and Lustig von Dom, was vast on both sides of the Atlantic.

DIVERSITY OF TYPE

One of the major bones of contention in recent years has been the diversity of type within the breed. Broadly speaking, the European dogs have evolved as a stockier type, with great emphasis being placed on head and mouth points, and perhaps more importance accorded to the forehand than the hindquarters. The Americans have favoured a more upstanding and stylish Boxer, with a cleaner head and slightly longer muzzle. Meanwhile, the British dogs, thanks to a wide variety of imports from both the USA and Europe, have tended to produce a more middle-of-the-road type of Boxer, which can frequently find favour with visiting judges from both continents.

Chapter Two

CHOOSING A PUPPY

The fact that you have bought this book suggests that you have decided that the Boxer is the breed for you. But is it? Only the most irresponsible of breeders will try to sell a puppy to a potentially unsuitable owner, so the chances are that you will be questioned (in some cases interrogated!) by the breeder you contact, as regards the likelihood of your making a responsible Boxer owner. So before you go in pursuit of your dream puppy, you must be absolutely positive in your own mind that this is the breed for you.

BREED CHARACTERISTICS
To begin with, let us look at the Boxer's sheer size. It is a medium to large breed, weighing anything between 55-70 lbs (25-32 kg), depending on sex, and measuring between 21-25 inches (53-63 cms) in height, so although described in its Breed Standard as a medium-sized dog, the Boxer has considerable bulk and strength.

The fact that the breed has a short foreface and well-padded muzzle means that the Boxer's smiling face will invariably conceal a goodly helping of saliva – or 'slobber' to the uninitiated. If you are house-proud, think twice before contemplating a Boxer. While essentially clean and quite fastidious in their habits, Boxers think nothing of having a good old shake and sending strings of slobber flying. The fact that they could land on your midnight-blue velvet curtains is to be considered!

Another aspect to be considered by would-be Boxer owners in Britain today is the fact that, while the general perception of the Boxer is of a breed with a short, stumpy tail and a bottom that wags ceaselessly, thanks to new legislation, fewer and fewer Boxer puppies are having their tails docked. This means that you may have to settle for a dog with a full, lashing tail, capable of clearing an entire coffee table in one wag! If you want a 'traditional-looking' Boxer, it is important to establish that the breeder you have contacted has had the puppies' tails docked.

TEMPERAMENT
The Boxer's temperament should always be beyond reproach. While he has many clown-like qualities and seems blessed with an acute sense of humour and fun, it should always be remembered that he has been bred down from stock which were versatile working and guard dogs. Consequently, a Boxer has a deep-seated instinct to protect his home and family, yet this should in no way make him provocative or quarrelsome.

The breed has great intelligence, with a brain which needs to be kept occupied. The Boxer thrives on company – human and canine – and no Boxer will flourish if

LEFT: The Boxer thrives on company – human and canine.

BELOW: You must decide if you want to show your Boxer, or if you are happy to keep him as a pet.

FACING PAGE: An older dog makes a wonderful companion, and is the ideal solution if you cannot cope with a puppy.

he is forced to spend long periods of time alone. He will, in the absence of any suitable mental stimulus, resort to making his own entertainment, and that could mean anything from taking down curtains to remodelling the new three-piece suite! Remember what is said about the Devil and idle hands, or paws in this case.

As with any dog, be it pedigree or mongrel, it is inadvisable to think of becoming a puppy owner unless there is likely to be someone at home virtually all day. Very few responsible breeders would consider selling one of their lovingly-reared puppies to a household where two partners are out at work all day.

Boxers are great family dogs and get on well with children, provided those children are taught firmly to respect them and do not abuse them in any way. Bringing up a child and a puppy together is beneficial to both and a dog should, in my opinion, be a compulsory part of any childhood, but I suppose I am biased.

EXERCISE NEEDS
Boxers are, like their namesakes, muscular animals and to keep in trim they need plenty of exercise of varying kinds. They benefit from both road work and free galloping, and although a vast garden is not essential, they do need an amount of space. There are always exceptions to the rule, and one of the fittest Boxers I know lives in a small house in central London. However, he is owned by two of the fittest people I know, and the dog gets parkland exercise at least four times a day.

The size and location of your home is incidental to your becoming a suitable Boxer owner. Provided your house and garden are totally secure, that you are prepared to exercise your Boxer regularly, come rain or shine, and that he will have company for most of the day, you and your Boxer could become an ideal partnership.

TRAINING TARGETS
Puppies do not teach themselves. If you are serious about becoming a Boxer owner, you must be prepared to school both yourself and your dog in basic disciplines. Your Boxer must be taught to come when he is called, to sit on command, and to go to his bed when told to. Boxer owners who neglect these vital disciplines early on in their puppies' lives rue the day, as very soon they find themselves with an unruly adolescent who has a very definite will of his own. Sadly, many such cases end up in rescue. Their only crime is having an owner who was too lazy to teach them basic good manners.

CHOOSING AN OLDER DOG
Most potential dog owners automatically think that the only route to dog ownership is through obtaining a puppy of nine weeks or thereabouts. They hold dear the mental image of the chocolate-box puppy who will grow with them, and develop the kind of personality they hope for. However, with that idyllic picture also goes the rigours of rearing and house-training.

For some people, particularly those who are not in the first flush of youth, it may be a better solution to give a home to an older dog. There are always Boxers in rescue through no fault of their own, and many of these make wonderful companions. It is almost as if they are so grateful to be given a second chance, they do their utmost to fit in and please their new owners.

There are also some breeders who prefer to place dogs they have finished showing or breeding from into 'retirement' pet homes. They believe that it is better for a dog who has done sterling work for them to finish his days in the lap of luxury as a pampered pet, rather than sit them out in a kennel situation. Such dogs may be as young as four years old and have another decade or so ahead of them, so unless you are adamant that you must have a puppy, why not consider one of these options?

DOG OR BITCH?

Having decided that a Boxer is the dog for you, you now need to establish whether you would prefer a dog or a bitch. There are pros and cons where both are concerned.

Male dogs do not come in season, but their hormones are nonetheless active, and a headstrong male with sex on his mind can prove something of an embarrassment if the object of his desires happens to be the vicar's ankle or your scatter cushions. On a more serious note, in a family with very young children, an over-zealous male Boxer could easily – if unintentionally – cause injury. Neutering the dog can be a solution, but castrated males tend to become overweight and may undergo a slight personality change.

Bitches usually come in season twice a year, causing a little mess around the house and the unwanted attraction of stray males, but they tend to be rather more affectionate and 'clinging' than the more independent males. Please, do not think of buying a bitch purely because you have the misguided idea that 'she can pay for herself' by having puppies. Forget it! Breeding dogs is for the dedicated, the knowledgeable, and the responsible.

When you have paid a not inconsiderable sum for your puppy, your mental arithmetic may tell you that she is not only cute, but she could be an investment if she has six puppies per litter. However, if you breed puppies properly, you will not make money. Believe me. I have yet to produce an in-the-black balance sheet for any litter of dogs I have bred – quite the reverse, in fact. If you wish to pursue breeding as a hobby, and are prepared to do it the right way, that is a different matter, but as for pin-money puppies, it's a non-starter.

To avoid the inconvenience of a bitch coming in season, treatments are available from the veterinarian to stop seasons. A bitch can be spayed, but, as with sterilised males, there is the tendency for neutered bitches to become overweight, unless their diet is regulated.

COLOUR

Every Boxer owner, past, present or future, has a favourite colour. Some owners always choose fawn dogs, others are equally passionate about brindles. Then there are whites, of course. Generally speaking, white Boxers are put to sleep at birth because there is the chance that their hearing may be impaired. Yet some people find whites attractive, and if a dog has coloured patches and is not albino, there is a strong possibility that the hearing will be in no way dysfunctional. Occasionally, breeders will rear a patched white puppy if they have a definite pet sale. However, such puppies are usually sold with no papers and on the strict understanding that they are never bred from.

The fawn colour varies from a pale, almost yellow fawn to a rich deer-red. The brindle coat pattern consists of a fawn ground colour with black stripes banding the

The male Boxer can be more difficult to handle than a bitch, although you avoid the problem of dealing with a seasonal cycle.

ABOVE: It is advisable to buy a tough, durable plastic dog bed, which cannot be chewed.

BELOW: Strainless steel feeding bowls are hard-wearing and easy to clean.

Photographs: Steve Nash.

entire coloured area. Strictly speaking, such stripes should be in distinct relief to the background colour, creating a 'tiger striped' effect. In reality, many Boxers are seen, often winning top honours, where brindling is so heavy that the first impression is that of an almost black dog.The next consideration is regarding a 'plain' or a 'flashy' dog. The Boxer Breed Standard dictates that up to one-third of the ground colour *may* be white, but in many countries fashion has decreed that the dogs who find favour in the show ring tend to be flashily marked, i.e. with white 'trim', usually consisting of white blaze, white flashes on the muzzle, white collar and 'shirt front', and four white socks. Few exhibitors persevere with solid-coloured Boxers (i.e. dogs devoid of any white markings) in the ring, feeling that they are handicapped under the majority of judges. 'Plain' dogs, however, are still seen winning in Germany and Central Europe.

This is sad, as conformational excellence should always be of greater importance than cosmetic aspects of the Boxer, and, importantly, plain bitches will be far less likely to produce white puppies than their flashier sisters. As a consequence of the show-ring appeal of flashy markings, many breeders immediately discard plain puppies as 'pet quality', even though, in truth, they may be anatomically superior Boxers to some of their more glamorous siblings. So when pet buyers arrive to view a litter, they may be offered only a choice of the plain puppies. However, many long-time Boxer owners may well remember owning a black-faced Boxer with little white, born before 'flashy' became the vogue.

FINDING THE RIGHT BREEDER

Hopefully, you and your Boxer are going to share more than a decade of your life together. You are going to become great pals and confidants, and your Boxer will become an important part of your family in every way. It therefore makes sense to spend some time making sure that you get the best possible puppy, and that you do everything in your power to avoid any problems.

Firstly, find a responsible breeder. The best way of doing this is by contacting your national Kennel Club, and asking for details of the Boxer Club in your area. Contact the secretary, explain that you are looking for a Boxer, and express an interest in joining the club. Do not rush into buying your Boxer. Ideally, you should attend a few functions at your local Boxer Club so that you have the chance to meet breeders. Go to a few shows, and talk to as many breeders as possible, concentrating on the kennels who are showing the kind of Boxers you admire. If you like their style, maybe they could be the breeder for you. When they have finished their day's exhibiting (and not before), approach them sympathetically, tell them exactly what you are looking for, and wait for the response. Beware the breeder who immediately, without enquiring about your circumstances, tells you that he/she has the perfect puppy for you. A far better bet is the breeder who gives you a card, and suggests you telephone in a few days' time when you can make an appointment to see the dogs at home. Before you even get invited to visit the dogs, the responsible breeder will have asked you all sorts of questions, some of which you may feel are tantamount to an invasion of your privacy. However, if you are keen to get one of those puppies, you will appreciate that the breeder has to be as sure as possible that you are a bona-fide buyer, who can give a puppy a loving and secure home for life. Answer all the breeder's questions honestly and frankly. If you are fair with them, they will be fair with you.

PET OR SHOW?

If you want a pet puppy, and have no intention of showing, say so, and remember that when, twelve months on, some well-meaning but self-appointed dog expert spots you walking your dog and says: "You ought to show him!" It is true that some great Champions have been discovered that way, but they are very, very few and far between. As for the talent-spotter's experience, you will probably discover that it goes no further than being able to tell one breed from another! There is nothing more infuriating for a breeder than to sell to a pet home a healthy, typical puppy, who may not be of top show quality due to some minor yet unimportant shortcoming, only to discover that the owner has been talked into showing it. Then, when the dog has not won and a judge has pointed out its faults, the owner gets irate with the breeder – who didn't sell it as a show prospect in the first place!

VISITING THE BREEDER

Telephone the breeder of your choice. Make an appointment to see the adult dogs. Keep the appointment and arrive on time. Dog breeders are very busy people and writing off an hour to entertain prospective customers means that other vital chores are delayed. Ask any questions about the dogs you feel you want answered, and don't worry about making yourself look silly. If you don't know, ask. Your breeder was once a rank novice, buying his first puppy. Asking now could avoid hours of trouble and worry at a later date.

Find out when the breeder expects to have a puppy available. Most reputable breeders have waiting lists, and puppies do not come to order. You may have to wait months, but do wait. Far too many puppy-buyers lose patience, snap up the first puppy they see advertised (regardless of its origins) and live to regret the day. If you are told that a puppy may be available from a specific litter, ask to see the dam of the puppies. If possible, ask to see the sire too, though there is every chance that he may not live at the same kennel, as most breeders travel to use the best available males, even though they might not own them.

If you are keen to buy a puppy from this breeder, and one is available soon, you may be asked to pay a deposit. This not only serves as a gesture of goodwill on your part, it tends to sort out the time-wasters who so often plague breeders. In due course, you get that long-awaited telephone call. You will have told the breeder of your preference as regards sex and colour. It is quite possible that a puppy is available, but it is not the sex or colour that you have set your heart on.

You will be asked to come and see the puppies anyhow. Think long and hard about this. Are you prepared to take a dog when you really want a bitch, or a brindle though you only like fawns? If you are not happy about taking an alternative, tell the breeder there and then that you would prefer to wait until he has another litter.

Do not go to see the available puppies. Why? Because you will come home with one, believe me! You will not be able to resist that face in the puppy pen, the black-faced brindle dog who looks up at you so longingly, with head on one side, almost knowing that you really wanted a flashy fawn bitch, but he is determined to win you over. It is true that there are often 'love matches' such as this, and the partnership remains a lifelong joy, but it is possible that you could later resent being emotionally blackmailed into taking something you didn't actually want.

LEFT: When your puppy first arrives home, he will probably feel rather lost and bewildered.

BELOW: Sleeping quarters will provide a safe, secure haven for the new arrival.

LEFT: Follow the breeder's recommended diet for the first few days. This will give your puppy a chance to settle in his new home. If you decide to change his food, do so gradually.

BELOW: While your puppy is feeding, occasionally take a piece of food from him. This will teach the pup not to get possessive over his food.

ASSESSING THE PUPPIES
When you arrive to see the puppies, ask politely if you can see the whole litter together. Stress that you realise that they are not all for sale, but explain that you would like to see them as a family, so to speak. This way you will get a good idea of the puppies in a relative sense. If the breeder sits you down in the kitchen, disappears to the kennel or nursery, then returns only to thrust a single puppy into your lap, it is impossible for you to know whether this puppy is half the size of its siblings or much more introvert than they are.

Hopefully, the breeder will be happy to oblige and show you the puppies in their playing area. The puppies should be in a clean, warm, comfortable environment. It should smell sweet, and the puppies should look well-fed and rounded (not pot-bellied, but pleasantly fat and chunky). They should appear happy and outgoing. Before you start falling in love with any one puppy, find out which puppies are available to you and forget the rest – immediately.

Another golden rule – if you see a puppy who appears timid and tries to run away when the others rush forward with eager anticipation, do not feel sorry for him and long to take him home and love him. This puppy may well have a temperament problem which will, should you choose to buy him, cause untold heartache in years to come. You want a bruiser of a puppy who is not afraid of anything – this is the sort of temperament you can channel and build on. Nervousness is not something you want to have to cope with.

Having been shown which puppies are available, concentrate on them and ask to see them apart from the unavailable puppies. Looking at the others will only cloud the issue. The breeder should be happy for you to handle the puppies, provided you have met with any requirements they may insist upon as regards disinfecting. Play with the puppies and see if one 'chooses' you. If there is such a puppy, then this is the one to take home. Dogs have wonderful instincts and are very quick to latch on to a character with whom they will be compatible. When a Boxer puppy chooses you in this way, you will be his for life.

I am assuming that you are buying your Boxer as a pet. If you are looking for a show prospect, there are a number of specialised technicalities to bear in mind, and there are much more detailed publications available for such buyers. However, here are a few tips worth remembering.

As well as being outgoing and well covered with flesh, a nicely-reared puppy should have a clear coat. Run your hand against the grain of the coat to check for fleas, scurf or any other skin problem. Check that the ears are clean and not foul-smelling or clogged with wax. When the puppy runs around, he should move freely and without effort, with a look of power, showing a firm, strong back and proud neck. Some people who are not used to seeing large numbers of very young Boxer puppies are sometimes concerned that they appear to have rather pointed heads! A very pronounced occiput is simply an indication of a very well-balanced head in adulthood, and not the result of an accident!

THE PAPERWORK
When you have decided on your puppy you will need to complete the transaction with the breeder by paying for the puppy and asking for a receipt. In the UK most good breeders will have their puppies insured, and this cover will remain in force for a week or so after the purchase date. This is not common practice in the USA. If

your puppy is insured, you will be given details of how you can take out extended cover, which I strongly recommend. Heaven forbid, but should you incur major veterinary expenses they can be crippling, and insurance is worth every penny.

You should also receive a copy of the dog's pedigree, details of his Kennel Club registration (if this has already been received by the breeder – if not, be sure to ask that the registration document is signed and forwarded immediately it is available), and a diet sheet along with instructions for inoculation. Most breeders will give you a supply of food to last a day or two, so that you avoid any drastic changes and risk an upset stomach.

COLLECTING YOUR PUPPY
Take a blanket and an old cardboard box with you when you collect your puppy. Place it on the back seat of the car, puppy inside, with someone sitting alongside to offer reassurance. This is probably your puppy's first car journey, so be prepared for him to be sick. Do not worry, it is a natural reaction. However, you are advised to be prepared and take some paper towels to clean up with.

ARRIVING HOME
When you get home, put your puppy straight into the garden where he may wish to relieve himself – if he has not already done so in the car! Give him time to acclimatise himself to the surroundings, sniffing around and exploring. Do not rush him, and do not invite the neighbours around for a viewing session. Leaving home will be enough of a trauma for the puppy for one day.

SLEEPING QUARTERS
You should have sorted out where your puppy is going to sleep – for the rest of his life – and that is where he should sleep from Day One. Do not weaken when he cries at night and smuggle him upstairs to the bedroom. If you do, you will be sorry! Every dog should have his own space, a place which is his and his alone, away from the general hubbub of the household, the kids and the television. This should be his retreat, his refuge.

Personally, I am a great advocate of the dog crate. Some pet owners see crates (which they invariably insist on calling 'cages' suggesting some zoo-like quality!) and immediately denounce them as being cruel. They are not. My advice is to invest in a crate which is large enough to house a fully-grown Boxer when standing up. The ideal type is made of heavy-duty metal mesh, with a hinged and lockable door to the front. They are not cheap, but being indestructible they are a once-in-a-lifetime purchase and will prove invaluable.

CRATE TRAINING
The crate should be situated in the place which is to be your Boxer's own area, ideally in a kitchen corner or utility area. The position should be warm and draught-free. The crate should be lined with newspaper in case of accidents. Place a heavy-duty cardboard box in the crate, with the front cut out to facilitate easy access. Put some old blankets and chewable but indestructible toys in the box, and leave your puppy in the box, crate locked, for ten minutes or so. He will cry and protest, but talk to him reassuringly and soothingly, without any physical contact. He will soon realise that you are not going to leave him, you are pleased with him, and after he

ABOVE: Supervise introductions with all members of the family – human and animal – to ensure your puppy becomes fully integrated.

BELOW: It is important that your puppy learns the 'house rules' from the very beginning. If he is allowed on the furniture when he is a puppy, you cannot reprimand him for climbing on the sofa when he is a an adult.

ABOVE: Remember, when you take on a puppy, you are responsible for his health and well-being throughout his entire life.

RIGHT: Meeting other dogs and other people is all part of the vital process of socialisation.

has done a ten-minute 'stretch', open the door, let him greet you, and you can cuddle him to your heart's content.

After your puppy's last meal before bedtime, put him straight into the garden and wait until he empties himself – and do wait, even if it takes an hour. Your puppy must learn from Day One to be clean after meals. Once he has obliged, lock him in his crate, and leave him there for the night without any contact whatsoever, no matter how much he objects. Giving in to his pathetic whining at this early stage will only make a rod for your own back.

The other excellent aspect of the crate is that dogs are naturally reluctant to soil their own beds. If they have free run of the kitchen they will think nothing of performing in a far corner, then retiring to their bed. If they have to foul just inches away from where they are sleeping, they will learn to control both bowel and bladder amazingly quickly.

Having settled your new Boxer puppy down for the night in his crate, it might be an idea for you to brew up a mug of hot chocolate – and prepare yourself for a sleepless night!

Chapter Three

CARING FOR YOUR BOXER

The Boxer is a relatively easily-maintained breed, requiring moderate exercise, a well-balanced diet, little by way of grooming, kind discipline and lots of tender loving care.

FEEDING
Your puppy's breeder should have given you a diet sheet, and this should not only include the meals at the age when you collect him, but right through into adulthood. Try to adhere to the diet sheet as closely as possible, but if, having read it, you feel that the recommended diet will not suit your lifestyle, discuss it with the breeder. Feeding dogs is no great mystery. Provided your Boxer receives a balanced diet, it will be easy for you to hit on a feeding regime which suits you both.

Today, the dog food industry is worth millions of pounds and dollars, and feeding techniques are becoming more and more sophisticated. Consequently, the market is overflowing with dog diets of different kinds, many of them promoted as 'complete' feeds. If a food purports to be complete, and this is borne out by your puppy's breeder, it should be respected as such. When you collect your puppy, you should decide whether or not you intend adopting this kind of feeding regime and, if so, confirm with the breeder that an appropriate complete feed is all that is necessary.

Not that many years ago, the majority of breeders fed what was basically a meat-and-biscuit combination. This did not satisfy all a dog's nutritional needs and, consequently, the basic diet was supplemented by calcium compounds during the growing stages, and various other additives thereafter.

These days highly qualified canine dieticians have taken the guesswork out of feeding. They have formulated a myriad of complex diets which contain all the necessary additives a dog needs at any given time of its life. They produce not only one complete feed, but a whole range within one product label. You will find today that most 'completes' have at least three grades of feeds: one for growth (suitable for puppies and youngsters who have yet to reach full maturity), one for high activity (for adult dogs who lead active lives), and one for lesser activity (for older dogs who need less energy due to their more sedentary lifestyle).

If you choose to feed a commercial brand of food, it is vitally important that you follow the manufacturer's instructions religiously. If the food is complete, it should need no additives at all, if you are feeding the correct level of diet. Many puppies are ruined, not through malnutrition as in past generations when rickets and the like were commonplace, but by over-enthusiastic owners who cannot resist the latest miracle 'supplement', brightly packaged on the pet-store shelf. You could do untold

ABOVE: As a dog gets older, feeding requirements may change. In their later years, most dogs prefer to have their rations split into two meals a day.

FACING PAGE
TOP: If you feed a complete diet, do not be tempted to add any supplements, as this will destroy the nutritional balance.

BOTTOM: The Boxer is a muscular dog and exercise, of varying sorts, is needed if the dog is to stay in prime condition.
Photos: Sheila Bowman.

damage to your puppy if you feed what should be a total diet, and then add calcium compounds, cod-liver oil, seaweed, brewer's yeast and heaven knows what on top! The best advice is to use the 'complete' diet recommended by your puppy's breeder – and do not meddle with it.

Many pet owners have the misguided belief that puppies have to be given cow's or goat's milk. Why? Is it natural for one animal to drink the milk of another? I have never fed milk to puppies, even when weaning. Once they have finished with their mother's milk, water should be all they need in the way of fluid. As soon as your puppy arrives home, he should have a heavy, non-spill water dish which should be checked regularly for a supply of clean, fresh water. This is doubly important if you are feeding a dry complete food, as some such products will tend to require an above average level of water.

The number of meals given per day should again be detailed in your Boxer puppy's diet sheet. Most puppies leave home when they are on about four meals per day, and eventually, by the time they are eighteen months old, they should be able to suffice with one meal a day. Many pet owners feel guilty about leaving their Boxers twenty-four hours between meals, and so prefer to give a light breakfast and a slightly reduced main meal later in the day. You should choose what suits you best, and stick to it. Dogs are very much creatures of habit and do not appreciate their feeding routine being upset. I currently have one elderly dog by whom you can set your watch – at 5p.m. each day, on the dot, she is standing over her feeding bowl in anticipation, and woe betide me if I am so much as five minutes late!

Give your Boxer puppy a cooked marrow-bone on which to gnaw, but avoid smaller bones which can splinter or be accidentally swallowed. Personally, I am reluctant to give cow hooves or rawhide chews at this stage, as there is a danger of the puppy swallowing bits which are too big for him to cope with. Dogs should always be supervised when they are given bones or any other type of chew.

From the very start you should decide where you are going to feed your Boxer, and ignore his pleading face at your own dinner table. Any attempt to jump up at the table must be swiftly corrected and the dog pushed into a sitting position – which must never be rewarded with a tasty morsel from your plate. Better still, when the human members of your family sit down to eat, give your Boxer the "Crate" command. In this way he will soon learn that the family dinner table is no concern of his, and he will be happy to take a nap at your mealtimes.

WORMING

When you collect your puppy from his breeder, he should have given you full details of his worming treatment to date. Most puppies get roundworms, but this is not a major problem if they are routinely treated. Give your puppy a day or two to settle in, and then take him to your local vet for a complete check-up. On this first visit, show the vet details of any wormings and ask for the suggested subsequent treatments. Be sure to carry your puppy into the waiting room and do not put him on the floor. He is still very vulnerable to disease, so be vigilant in this respect.

These days excellent and evidently palatable worming pastes have tended to replace those protracted treatments which entailed several pills being pushed down disapproving puppies' throats!

Some worming treatments will dissolve worms before they are expelled, but it may be that some worms will be passed. It is advisable to check stools as you carry out your daily clean-up, a habit which you – as a responsible Boxer owner – will have already acquired. Be sure to dispose of stools efficiently, either by burning or by flushing into a main sewer.

Worming should be carried out on a routine basis, twice yearly, as well as at any other time when you suspect that your Boxer may have a worm infestation.

INOCULATIONS

It is imperative that your Boxer puppy is inoculated against distemper, leptospirosis, hepatitis and parvovirus. Nowadays, the most favoured inoculation consists of a two-shot course, the first being given around twelve weeks of age and the second some two weeks later. Veterinarians will vary slightly in their preferred age, but twelve weeks for the first injection seems the general rule of thumb.

Following completion of the first set of inoculations, you will be given a vaccination certificate which should be kept in a safe place. In fact, it is as well to keep all your Boxer's 'paperwork' in the same place as other important family documents. All too easily, they can get stuffed in the back of a drawer and can never be found when they may be required, sometimes urgently.

Your vet will notify you annually when your Boxer requires a booster shot, and on those visits most vets will automatically give such patients a routine thorough check-up when any major health problems will be spotted.

Some may recommend an inoculation against kennel cough. Should you envisage putting your Boxer into a boarding kennel at some stage, the kennel may insist on this in addition to the standard inoculations, so it is as well to be prepared. This will also be recorded on your dog's vaccination certificate, and the importance of keeping this certificate safe will be appreciated when the boarding kennel owner asks to see it when you check your dog in. Without it, few kennels will accept a boarder.

HOUSING

I have already stressed the value of training your Boxer to sleep in a crate, and getting him used to being put in the crate whenever you feel it is necessary. This assumes that your Boxer is going to be essentially a house-dog as opposed to a kennel-dog.

No dog thrives in a kennel alone, and I cannot recommend investing in a kennel and run if you own just one Boxer. In the first place such a building, no matter how modest, will be very expensive. Secondly, even though you might set out intending your Boxer to spend some time each day in the kennel, in reality he will end up in the house. Two dogs together, however, are a different matter and they will enjoy their time, free of humans, doing doggy things together. They will, nonetheless, appreciate their time spent in the house with the family.

EXERCISE

Many Boxer owners make the fatal mistake of thinking that their growing puppy needs vast amounts of exercise to help him grow big and strong. In truth, those growing bones are actually quite delicate, and for the first six months of his life your Boxer puppy's exercise should be restricted to playing in your garden. During this time he can become accustomed to his lead and collar, and you can begin basic training (See Chapter Four).

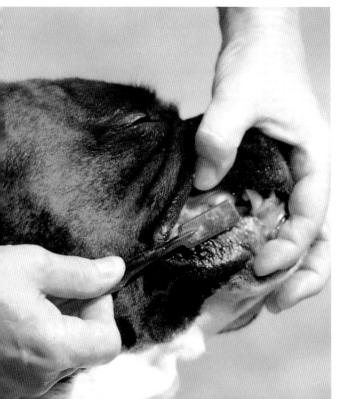

ABOVE: The Boxer is one of the easiest breeds to care for. The short coat needs no more than regular grooming to keep it clean and shining.

LEFT: Your Boxer should get used to having his teeth cleaned from an early stage.

ABOVE: If wax accumulates in the ears, they should be gently cleaned with cotton-wool.

RIGHT: Exercise on hard surfaces will keep your dog's nails short, but sometimes you will need to take further action. Make sure you only trim the end of the nail and do not cut into the quick.

If you do not have a large enough garden, small gentle walks to the park will suffice. Long sustained walks and galloping sessions should only be started after six months, and then introduced very gradually if you are not to do more harm than good.

GROOMING

The Boxer is one of the easiest breeds to groom, with his short, close and shining coat. It is a good idea to get your Boxer puppy used to being handled in a weekly maintenance check. Not only will this assure you that he is clean and healthy, but it will prepare him for future close inspections by veterinarians or – who knows? – by dog show judges.

TEETH

Make your puppy show you his teeth, and do not take "No" for an answer. Start this routine when your puppy is small and he has no choice in the matter. After all, you are the boss. Vets can get a little impatient with boisterous adult Boxers who have never been taught to have their mouths opened, and tempers can run high. Plenty of chewing on big marrow-bones should help keep your Boxer's teeth clean and free of tartar – this is particularly important if you are feeding a complete diet where no real grinding is called for.

From a very early age get your Boxer used to having his teeth cleaned with a proprietary dog toothpaste. This should be applied with a harsh toothbrush, but be careful not to make the gums bleed in your enthusiasm.

EYES

Your Boxer's eyes should sparkle with health, and the only area to watch here is the inner corners from which may come a slight tear-stain. A weekly swab with luke-warm water and cotton-wool should keep this in check. Make sure that any folds of skin around the muzzle are always dried thoroughly after bathing. Severe staining can be treated with proprietary products specially designed for the purpose.

EARS

Ears should be inspected, and they should appear clean, free from acute odour and showing no great build-up of wax. If wax is apparent, the ears should be gently cleaned with cotton-wool, and some ear drops should be administered. Ask your vet to recommend a suitable product. Avoid the temptation to probe into the ears with cotton buds as you may do some serious damage.

NAILS

Nails should be kept short. Plenty of walking on concrete should keep them in trim, but sometimes it may be necessary to cut them. To this day, cutting a dog's nails is the one job I absolutely hate, as do my dogs! But it has to be done. I find the guillotine type of nail-clippers the easiest to use.

It is imperative that you start trimming nails when your puppy is small and manageable. Just trim a sliver off the end, making sure that you avoid the quick. If you are of faint heart, leave nail-cutting to your vet, but still get your puppy used to the routine from an early age.

COAT CARE

As regards grooming, all your Boxer needs is a weekly rub down, ideally with a rubber grooming mitt. This is made of heavy-duty rubber, studded on one side. It not only gently drags out loose and dead hairs, but it also helps to massage your Boxer and tone him up, making him feel really on top of the world. For smartness, his white trim, if he has such, can always be enhanced with the aid of a chalk block.

Sometimes you may notice a little dry skin, causing dandruff or scurf. The cause of this is probably dietary, and a little margarine added to the food will probably clear it up. If it persists, consult your vet.

Even in the most fastidious of households, dogs can pick up fleas. During your weekly grooming sessions, always run your hand against the grain of the coat to check for any unwanted passengers. If you find any such parasite, bath your Boxer in a suitable insecticidal shampoo and monitor the situation on a daily basis. Make sure that bedding is also treated.

Dogs that live in the countryside where livestock graze may pick up the occasional tick. These parasites fasten themselves on to the dog's skin by a mouth-piece and suck blood. They must not be pulled out, as you will probably leave the mouth-piece embedded in the dog's skin, and this will eventually cause an abscess. To remove a tick, soak some cotton-wool in a mild disinfectant and the tick will then release its hold and will come away intact.

BATHING

There should be no need to bath your Boxer more than twice a year if he is regularly groomed, but some Boxers have a nasty habit of rolling in all manner of unpleasant things, and in such cases, a bath is the only answer. Just as with nail-clipping and mouth-opening, my advice is to give your Boxer his first bath when he is about sixteen weeks old, and small enough to restrain if he happens to freak out at his first sight of a shower nozzle. The prospect of a fully-grown male Boxer being hauled into, and out of, a bath for the first time ever is truly daunting.

SUMMARY

Try to get into the habit of giving your Boxer his weekly once-over at the same time on the same day. Be firm in your handling, but make it a fun time for you both, and afterwards be sure to follow it with a game. In this way you will find that your Boxer soon realises that it pays to be beautiful – and can be fun too!

The correct way to put on a check-chain. The lead ring is on the right-hand side of the neck, with the ring pulling downwards when the lead is tightened, so that it releases automatically.

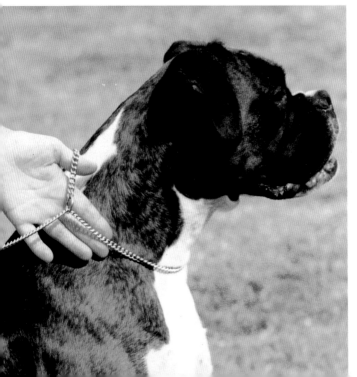

Incorrect: The check-chain will not release automatically.

Chapter Four

TRAINING YOUR BOXER

The Boxer is a highly intelligent breed whose physical conformation, steady temperament and great brain capacity make him a versatile dog who can 'turn his hand' to a wide variety of tasks. Boxers have been trained to a remarkably high level to fulfil specialist roles with the armed and police forces, they have served as guide dogs, and in competition work they have acquitted themselves well at both Working Trial and Championship Obedience level. Currently, Agility is a growing sport, and the Boxer's boundless energy and inherent sense of fun make him a perfect Agility dog.

As your Boxer puppy grows up, you may wish to get involved in specialised activities, but, to begin with, you will be aiming for a moderate level of obedience which will ensure that your dog is well acquainted with the social graces, and is a pleasure to live with. Training a Boxer puppy to such a standard is well within the capabilities of the average dog owner, as so much training is basic common sense.

The Boxer is an intelligent dog who will respond well to training.

After you have completed your basic training, you may wish to progress further by attending Obedience or Ringcraft (show training) classes. If you want to get involved in Agility training, you must wait until your dog is over twelve months of age before starting, as it is potentially dangerous to subject a growing dog to the exertion of jumping over obstacles. Details of all training classes will be passed on by your national Kennel Club. Alternatively your veterinarian may be aware of classes and instructors in your area.

HOUSE-TRAINING

Your basic training will obviously begin with house-training. Your Boxer must be taught that fouling indoors is not allowed, and, happily, Boxers very soon become 'clean'.

Firstly, when you get up in the morning, be sure to let your Boxer puppy out into the garden, or whatever area you have decided is acceptable as his toilet. Watch over him until he has 'performed' and then make a big fuss of him. When your puppy has finished eating a meal – any meal – put him out again, watching until he has done the necessary, always rewarding with praise. Last thing at night, your puppy should be given the last chance of the day to relieve himself before bedtime. If you get into the habit of toileting your puppy first thing in the morning, after every meal, and last thing at night, he will soon become spotlessly clean in the house.

Inevitably there will be the odd accident. If the puppy produces an indoor puddle or pile in your company, and you see it happening, scold him with a loud and firm "No!" and immediately put him out into his designated toilet area. If, however, you find a mistake which the puppy has obviously left earlier, it is pointless scolding the puppy, as he will not associate his earlier wrongdoing with your present ill temper. He will presume that you are cross with him for whatever he is doing at that precise moment, which could be lying down quite peacefully.

Similarly, if you find a soiled bed in the morning (which will be unusual if you follow my advice and crate-train), shouting at the puppy will have no effect, for the very same reason. Correction can only be productive if it is implemented instantly.

CORRECTIVE TRAINING

From an early age your puppy will, from time to time, do something which he should not. When teething, there will be the temptation to chew anything and everything. Make sure that your puppy has plenty of toys on which he can have a good gnaw. It is important that your puppy is given his own toys. The old-fashioned idea of giving a puppy an old slipper is a stupid one. If it's okay to chew an old slipper, why would it not be equally acceptable to tackle a brand new pair of shoes? To the puppy, there will be little difference.

Your Boxer puppy will quickly realise that he is part of your family if he is properly treated. Boxers are natural 'people dogs', so it follows that your puppy will want to be with you. He may well attempt to get up on the furniture and share your armchair when you are watching television. Bouncing a ten-week-old puppy on your lap may be fun, but will you be that keen on the idea when he is fully grown? Even a well-groomed Boxer will lose hair, and you may not want dog hairs on your furniture. Therefore, it is essential from the start to establish what is acceptable, and what is not. Your Boxer should be clear in his own mind which places are out of bounds.

Personally, I recommend a dog-bed of some sort, placed near your own furniture, or at the side of the fireplace (dogs naturally love to get near the heat). I find the foam-walled, oval-shaped beds with detachable and washable covers are ideal for this purpose. When you are relaxing, the puppy can be placed in such a bed, with a few toys, and he will soon get the message.

When your Boxer puppy starts to chew something which is forbidden, when he tries to leap on to the sofa, or contemplates any other misdemeanour, a short, loud, firm "No!", with perhaps a gentle tap on the nose, should be sufficient to convey your displeasure. If your puppy fails to get the message, you must be more firm and exert your authority. However, it is important to remain calm, and never lose your temper. Boxers may appear to be tough and boisterous, but, in fact, they are quite sensitive dogs.

LEAD TRAINING
From an early age your Boxer puppy must be introduced to a collar and lead. I do not agree with keeping a collar on a dog all the time, as I believe it could be potentially dangerous. However, this is a matter of choice.When you are away from home, your dog must be on the lead at all times and, if you are able to find a secure open space where he can run free, then he should always wear a collar bearing your home telephone number.

Start off with a light leather or nylon adjustable collar. Put it on your puppy when you are about to start a game. He should not be unduly worried by it, and if he is a little wary, your game will soon distract him. Each day, give your puppy a ten-minute session wearing the collar until he is totally relaxed about it.

The next step is to attach a lead to the collar during your play sessions, just allowing it to trail behind. In this way, your Boxer will soon get used to the sense of something beyond the collar. Once he is quite unconcerned by the lead, you can begin to hold it. To begin with, simply follow your puppy around the garden, letting him take the lead, so to speak. After a few sessions like this, you can begin to introduce a little discipline. Walk in a straight line, with your puppy at your left side. If he tugs, jerk him back into position, using a tidbit as enticement if necessary.

Check-chains, or slip chains, can be used effectively on puppies, but they must be of the larger-link type. The fine chains can cause injury when used as a training aid. It is also important that the check-chain is put on correctly, with the lead ring on the right-hand side of the neck, the ring pulling upwards when the lead is tightened, so that it releases automatically. I recommend using a good check-chain and a strong leather lead when walking your adult Boxer, as this will give you maximum control.

With practice, your puppy will soon get used to walking at your side, and for this exercise the standard "Heel" command can be used. In conjunction with this routine lead training, further commands of "Right", "Left" and "Stop" can be implemented, their use being self-explanatory. All the basic lead training should be done at home or in a quiet area, free of distractions. It is inadvisable to introduce your Boxer to town and traffic before he is lead-trained. The consequences could be most unfortunate.

THE SIT
A dog which will sit on command is a pleasure to have around and will never make a nuisance of itself. Teaching a dog to sit can be done quite simply with example and

ABOVE: To begin with, you will have to handle your Boxer to show him what is required.

ABOVE: A slight pressure on the hindquarters will ease your dog into the Sit position.

LEFT: Hold your dog in the Sit position for a few moments, and give plenty of praise.

TEACHING THE DOWN

A food treat is a great incentive with a Boxer. Hold the treat at ground level and give a sharp, downward tug with the lead.

The dog should go into the Down position, his nose following the tidbit.

Hold your dog in the Down position, and reward with the tidbit.

reward. Boxers enjoy their food and an edible 'prize' at the end of a successful training session will soon get the message across.

An excellent time to begin teaching the Sit is just prior to mealtimes. Place one hand on the dog's throat, put the other on his rear, just in front of his tail, and push down gently, giving the clear command "Sit". Hold the puppy in the sitting position for a few moments, repeating the command. Release and praise him, then give him a mouthful of his meal. Repeat the process two or three times, then let him finish the rest of his meal in peace.

After a week or so, you should find that your puppy will oblige when given the command to sit without your needing to handle him. When he seems proficient at this, continue the process, gradually distancing yourself further and further away from your Boxer. Regular training sessions should be kept up well into maturity.

THE STAY
Once your puppy has mastered the Sit, you can introduce the Stay. Start off with your puppy in the Sit, and stand facing him, just a few feet away. Repeat the "Stay" command as you gradually take a few paces back. Your puppy should remain in the Stay for a few moments when you have come to a standstill. Then you can give the "Come" command, or simply call his name, and he should bound towards you in anticipation of your forthcoming praise.

Teaching the Stay can be speeded up if you employ the help of a friend or another family member. Your assistant can stand behind the puppy, holding him on the lead. In this way, any attempts to break the Stay before he receives your command will be thwarted. Once you have given the command "Come", your assistant can release the dog.

THE DOWN
This is a useful exercise to teach, as if you are ever in an emergency situation, a quick response to the command "Down" could be a life-saver.

Start off with your dog on the lead in the Sit, at your left side. Give the command "Down" and give a sharp downward tug on the lead, at the same time applying gently pressure on the dog's shoulder. Use a deep, firm tone of voice, and your puppy will soon understand what is required. As you repeat the exercise, you can give the verbal command without the manual aids.

The secret to successful basic training is little and often. Do not leave your puppy for four days and then attempt an hour-long session. Your Boxer will lose all sense of continuity and get bored during the irregular training. Make it fun for both of you, always ending with a ball game or something your Boxer really enjoys.

SHOW TRAINING
If your Boxer puppy matures into an excellent example of his breed, you may wish to try your hand at showing him. If you do, you should start at the lowest level with a Match or Exemption show. These are usually held in conjunction with larger general shows, or arranged specifically as fund-raising events for a local charity.

In order to avoid potential embarrassment, your Boxer will need to be trained for the show ring. In beauty shows, there is no need for your Boxer to sit. He must learn how to stand in the traditional show pose, displaying the typical Boxer outline. He must also be happy about the judge examining his mouth, handling the rest of his body, and – in the case of males – checking his testicles. From an early age your puppy must get used to strangers handling him in this way.

To stand or 'set up' your Boxer, firstly put one hand under his neck, the other under his brisket (the forepart of the body, between the chest and forelegs). Gently lift the dog up under the brisket so that his feet are just off the ground, and slowly drop him into position so that his front legs are well under him, and are set parallel when looking at the dog head-on. Keeping one hand under the neck, so that his head remains proud and high, run your other hand down the back of the neck, and along the back in a stroking motion. Gently lift up the hindquarters and drop them back into position so that the angulation of the stifles is noticeable, and the hocks are at 90 degrees to the ground. Your Boxer should always hold his tail high, but if he finds all this mauling about a little daunting you can encourage him by just tickling the underside of his tail which should have the desired effect.

Hold your Boxer in this position, talking quietly and reassuringly to him all the time. You should always use a check-chain for showing, though perhaps a slightly smaller-linked chain than your training collar. When doing this 'setting up' training at home, ask a neighbour or someone the dog does not know intimately, to come along and 'judge' him, opening his mouth and handling even his most sensitive bits!

The next stage is to move your Boxer as you would in the show ring. The pace is important, and you should get your Boxer used to moving alongside you at a well co-ordinated trot. This is faster than a walk, but not at such a speed that the dog easily breaks stride. He should be taught to move at this pace in a straight line, in a triangle and in a circle. At the end of the moving, your Boxer should also be taught to stand free on a loose lead, ideally with his legs reverting naturally to the same position as when you stacked him.

This comes with practice, and a Boxer will always be seen at his best when standing at the end of a loose lead, with his attention captured by something intriguing in the distance. Boxer exhibitors are notorious for throwing 'attention-getters' in the ring, these varying from chunks of garlic-flavoured baked liver to rabbits' feet, along with the ubiquitous squeaky ball! Take my advice, and do not attempt to 'throw'. It is not necessary if your Boxer is well schooled.

When a pet Boxer goes into a show ring environment for the first time, a major problem that is often experienced is that the dog is not used to standing nose-to-tail with other dogs, and, despite your religious training efforts, his concentration wanders to the new-found friends he has discovered on either side of him. This can be helped by getting friends to bring their dogs to your home for mock show sessions. However, it is far better to attend a Ringcraft class where experienced handlers will give you excellent advice, and school your dog in what is essentially an authentic show environment.

TRAINING FOR THE COMMUNITY

You have now trained your young Boxer to be a model of decorum; he is obedient and a pleasure to be with. There may be many people in your own community who would love to be able to share their life with a dog, but, through no fault of their own, they cannot. These may be hospitalised children, young people with learning difficulties at residential homes, or the elderly who may have been forced to give up their own homes, and possibly their pets.

There are several charitable organisations which are always happy to accept new

The golden rule is to keep training sessions short and to make them fun. In this way the dog enjoys what he is doing and retains concentration.

ABOVE: The Stay is a very useful exercise to learn. In the early stages of training, a hand-signal will help your Boxer to understand what is required.

BELOW: The versatile Boxer can be trained to compete in Agility and Working Trials.
Photo: Sheila Bowman.

dogs and owners on to their books so that they may become part of a visiting scheme. Prior to acceptance, your Boxer will have to be tested for character and temperament. If you do become involved in one of these schemes, you will derive enormous satisfaction from seeing how much pleasure your very own Boxer can bring to the less fortunate. It can be a most rewarding exercise.

You should always remember that you are privileged to be a Boxer owner, and that you have a responsibility to maintain the breed's reputation. Your Boxer should be a great advertisement for the breed, with sound temperament and impeccable manners. With correct and thorough training, your Boxer should bring joy to everyone he meets and act as an ambassador par excellence. The breed has a great and noble heritage of which you should be proud. You owe it to your dog, and the breed, to ensure that he preserves the good name of the Boxer breed.

Chapter Five

SHOWING YOUR BOXER

For the purposes of this chapter, I will assume that your Boxer is a typical example of his breed, has an above-average level of quality, and you have decided to get further involved in showing. In theory, dog shows exist as competitive vehicles at which potential breeding stock can be assessed and evaluated. Through showing, breeders can meet up at regular intervals to study the dogs that are currently being campaigned, and to evaluate the faults and virtues being produced in certain bloodlines. By studying the state of the breed via the show ring, they can plan their breeding programmes accordingly.

In truth, the vast majority of people who show dogs today are hobby-exhibitors, owning just one or two dogs who are primarily companions. In dog showing they have found a hobby which is still relatively inexpensive, and through which they can meet new friends who share a common interest.

To begin with, let me appear quite brutal. You have decided to show your Boxer, but is he really good enough? Once you start to put him up against other dogs, minor faults which to you – as his devoted owner – are quite irrelevant, will be focused on by judges and other rival exhibitors. You might find this hurtful. You love your Boxer. He is a great pal and protector. Do you really want to subject him to what could be seen as the indignities of the show ring? If you can appreciate that your Boxer is less than perfect, and can cope with constructive criticism of your pride and joy, then by all means go ahead. But do think long and hard before you start spending your money on entry fees.

If you are determined to show, and your dog's breeder has told you that your dog has developed into a show-quality specimen, you are well advised to start on the bottom rung. Try your luck at the smaller events, and give yourself the opportunity to find your feet before you contemplate entering one of the major shows where the cream of the breed will be competing for top awards.

When you show your Boxer, the judge will be evaluating him against the Breed Standard. This is the written description of the perfect specimen, detailing, point by point, what constitutes the ideal Boxer. Your dog will be measured against this, and then assessed alongside the competition in your class.

ANALYSING THE BREED STANDARD
The first thing any judge will be looking for is the overall appearance of a dog. The Boxer should be a noble dog, squarely built, with strong bone and great musculation. He should have an outline which is typical of his breed, and he should also have a typical head, for it is the head which makes the Boxer quite unique with all its

Andrew Brace is pictured judging at Monmouth County Kennel Club, USA, in 1993, awarding Best of Breed in Boxers to Ch. Hi-Tech's Arbitrage, owned by Bill and Tina Truesdale and handled by Kimberly Pastella. Arbitrage was the Top Working Dog of all breeds in the USA for 1993, and the following year he won the Working Group at the prestigious Westminster Kennel Club show.

ABOVE: If you have ambitions to show your Boxer, you must start training from an early age. This puppy is being taught to stand in the Boxer's traditional show pose.

BELOW: At nine months of age, this Boxer is fulfilling his early potential. You must be objective about your dog's virtues and faults if you want to compete at the highest level.

complexities. The Boxer should be fearless yet biddable and always convey the impression of being self-assured. In the show ring he should almost have a 'swagger' about him, giving off an aura which lets you know that at least he knows he is the best.

HEAD

The Boxer's head is a very important aspect of the dog. While judging should always be based on the overall picture, no matter how outstanding a Boxer is in construction and movement, if he has a head like a plank, he can never be a good Boxer.

The head should be in proportion to the body. In other words, a Boxer should not look 'heavy headed', but any suggestion of lightness or insignificance about the head is equally wrong. The skull is clean and lean, without bulging cheeks. The muzzle is broad and deep, and should always appear powerful. It must never be too short, too long, too narrow or shallow, or too mean or pointed. The skull and muzzle must be in balance, the whole head being almost brick-like. The skull should be cleanly covered with tight-fitting skin, with no wrinkle on the forehead when the dog is relaxed. When the dog is alert, a slight wrinkle will appear. There are constant creases down the side of the muzzle, running from the base of the muzzle.

The black facial mask must be confined to the muzzle, and should never creep up over the eyes as this creates a dour and sombre expression. The black mask should be present even when the muzzle is flashed with white. The lower jaw is slightly undershot and curves slightly upward with a gentle sweep. Most breeds of dog insist on what is known as a 'scissor' bite, with the upper teeth closely fitting over the lower. However, as a result of the Boxer's Bulldog ancestry, the bite is slightly undershot, with the lower incisors protruding beyond the upper. The upper jaw is very broad where it joins the skull, and tapers very slightly to the nose.

The muzzle shape is enhanced by very thick, well-padded upper lips. The impression of width is helped by the fact that these padded lips are supported by the wide-set canine teeth of the lower jaw. The lower edge of the upper lip should rest exactly on the edge of the lower lip, emphasising great strength and depth of chin. Only with this correct lip-to-lip placement and good depth of chin will a Boxer have that wonderfully snooty, aristocratic expression. A weak chin creates a 'frog face', totally devoid of arrogance. A too-pronounced underjaw, where the lower teeth are visible, creates a menacing look.

The top of the Boxer's skull is slightly arched, but not rounded or dead flat. The occiput (the back point of the skull) is detectable but should not be pronounced. There is a distinct stop, i.e. where the skull and muzzle meet in profile, and there should be a definite rise of skull. A flat skull will give a Boxer a rather plain head. The length of the muzzle should be such that the distance from the nose tip to the inside corner of the eye is one-third of the distance from the nose tip to the occiput. The nose should be tilted upwards, so that the tip is always higher than the level of the root of the muzzle. The nose must be broad and black, with wide nostrils, and a distinct line should be seen between the nostrils.

EYES

One of the most beautiful aspects of the Boxer's head should be its eyes. They should be dark brown, forward-looking, and never too small or deep-set. Yet they should never be bolting. The eyes should be full enough to convey great fire and intelligence, and indicate great character, their shape being between round and almond. The eye rims should be dark, and the haw – or third eyelid – should not show. While the Breed Standard does not actually mention the colour of the haw, fully pigmented third-eyelids will be essential in a really excellent Boxer head, for unpigmented (pink) haws can create a rather wild expression. Light eyes will detract from an otherwise good Boxer head, so dark brown is the ideal.

EARS
In the USA and some European countries, the ears are traditionally cropped. This entails cutting off the edges on two sides of a puppy's ear, and taping them up in frames, when the Boxer is quite young. This trains the ears to stand erect. The practice is outlawed in Britain. A cropped ear will always enhance the 'alertness' of a dog, and can create the illusion of a cleaner skull than would be the case with natural ears.

Natural ears should be of moderate size, thin, and set wide apart on the highest part of the skull. They should lie flat and close to the cheek when the Boxer is relaxed, but fall forward with a distinct crease when he is alert. Sometimes a 'rose' ear is seen in Boxers. This is a Bulldog-type ear where the ear is folded backwards and carried behind the skull. It is an ugly fault, but, thankfully, not often seen in the show ring today.

MOUTH
The Boxer has an undershot jaw, the canine teeth – or tusks – are set wide apart, with the six incisors between set in a dead straight line in the bottom jaw, and set in a line which curves slightly forward in the upper jaw. The teeth should be strong and the bite powerful. Boxer mouths, on the whole, are not good. Wry mouths are commonplace. This is a condition where the lower jaw is crooked, set in such a way that if you were to draw a vertical line down the centre of the foreface, the relative position of the upper and lower canines would be different on the right from the left. In other words, the left side would not mirror the right, which would be the case in a perfect Boxer head. Rounded, narrow underjaws are also a common fault.

NECK
The Boxer's neck is round, of ample length to convey dignity and nobility, strong, muscular and tight-skinned. It should be clean, showing no dewlap (excess skin under the throat). There should be a distinctly marked nape, and the whole neck should arch elegantly down to the withers (the highest part of the body, immediately behind the neck).

FOREQUARTERS
The shoulders should be long and sloping, lie close, and not be over-muscled. The upper arm is long and makes an approximate right angle with the shoulder blade. From the front, the forelegs should be straight, parallel and of strong bone. The elbows should not stand off the chest wall, as seen in the Bulldog, but neither should they be so close as to create a 'terrier front'. The forearms are perpendicular, long and firmly muscled, while the short pasterns should be clearly defined, and very slightly slanted.

*Ch. Norwatch
Sunhawk
Wanneroo:
Natural,
uncropped ears
give a more
gentle
expression.*

*The well-
padded upper
lips contribute
to the Boxer's
unique facial
expression.*

Cropped ears change the overall expression of the Boxer. The practice of ear-cropping is banned in Britain.

Photo: Eddie Banks

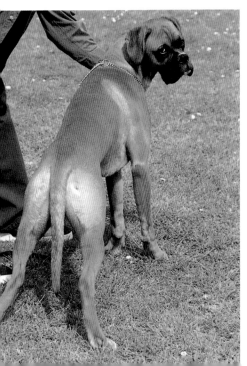

LEFT: An undocked tail: Traditionally, the Boxer is shown with a docked tail, but legislation may change this in the future.

BODY

The Boxer must present a square profile, and the chest should be deep, reaching to the elbows. The depth of the chest should be half the height at the withers, and the ribs should be well sprung and extend well back towards the loin. The withers are clearly defined, and the back should be broad and strongly muscled, short, straight, yet slightly sloping downwards towards the tail-set. The loin is short, well tucked up underneath and taut. The underline of the Boxer should show gradual tuck-up, the lower abdominal line blending into a curve towards the rear.

HINDQUARTERS

The Boxer's hindquarters should be strong, well-muscled and really 'hammy', the muscles standing out almost plastically from under the skin. The thighs are long, broad and curved, with good development of the second thigh. The broad croup (rump) is slightly sloped and the pelvis should be long and broad. There should be good angulation behind, but not excessively so. Over-angulation will create weak movement which lacks power and drive. The stifles (the joint of the hindleg between the thigh and second thigh) should not be straight, but this may not be as detrimental to movement as the other extreme. The hocks (the collection of bones of the hindleg forming the joint between the second thigh and metatarsus) should be quite short.

FEET

The ideal forefoot should be small and cat-like, with well arched toes and hard pads. The hind feet tend to be slightly longer.

TAIL

The Boxer's tail is customarily docked, but in Britain legislation has decreed that it is illegal for lay persons to dock tails. Fewer veterinarians seem prepared to carry out this simple operation, so the chances are that Boxers with full tails may become quite commonplace. The British Kennel Club has yet to make any statement as to what should be considered the correct length and carriage of a complete tail, and in my experience they vary dramatically.

MOVEMENT

The Boxer's movement should immediately create the impression of power and nobility. He should have excellent reach in front, without picking the forefeet up too high, and tremendous drive behind. The profile action should be totally effortless and ground-covering. Coming on, the Boxer's front action should be clean and true, the forefeet converging as speed increases. Going away, the Boxer's driving hindquarters should move in such a way that the hocks appear parallel.

COAT

The show Boxer may be fawn or brindle, with white markings being acceptable if no more than one-third of the base colour. Fawn can vary from an almost yellow fawn to a rich deer-red. Brindle should consist of clear black stripes on a fawn background, the stripes running parallel to the ribs all over the body. The stripes should contrast distinctly to the base colour, being neither too close nor too sparsely dispersed. Many brindles are badly marked, some appearing almost black. These 'black brindles' do not seem to be penalised by judges, and the colour is indeed proving very popular!

SIZE
The Boxer male should be between 22.5 and 25 inches (57-63 cms), while a bitch should be between 21 and 23 inches (53-59 cms), these measurements being taken at the shoulder. In weight, Boxer males will tip the scales at 66-70 lbs (30-32 kg), with bitches 25-27 kg.

SUMMARY
So, there you have it. Sounds terribly complicated, doesn't it? I suspect that you may have read through the Breed Standard, checked every aspect of your beloved Boxer against it, and concluded that he is perfect! Most people do, but interpreting and applying the Standard takes years of experience. If you are to get pleasure from your showing, you must be able to understand all the subtleties of the Breed Standard, and should be able to work out why one dog beats another, though sometimes I have to admit it isn't that obvious from ringside!

Your knowledge of the Boxer can be increased and improved through reading as much available literature as possible. There have been many excellent books written on the breed – read every one if you possibly can. You can also ask the more experienced breeders and exhibitors to explain anything which you might not fully understand. If they are not too busy, most will be happy to give you their time, encouraged by the fact that you are prepared to admit that you don't already know it all!

Sit at the ringside to watch the judging, and try to establish what are the good points about each of the dogs. Any fool can find faults. It takes a connoisseur to appreciate virtues, and with experience will come the eye to evaluate those important intangibles such as balance, quality and style.

SHOW EQUIPMENT
In your show bag you will need the following:
Show lead and slip chain.
Grooming glove.
Chamois leather and coat dressing (for a last-minute shine).
Chalk block or dry-shampoo (should white socks get muddy on the way to the ring).
A bag of tidbits, for emergencies (and not to be used to distract the opposition in any way!)
Benching chain and blanket (if the show is benched).
Crate and blanket (if the show is not benched).
Exhibitor's clip for holding your ring number.
Pooper-scoopers or disposal bags.
Bottle of drinking water, and bowl.
Plastic spray bottle (to keep your Boxer cool if it is a really hot day).

AT THE SHOW
Get to the show early, giving yourself a good half-hour before judging is due to start. Bench or crate your dog, then buy a catalogue so that you can check your dog is

SHOW PREPARATION

The Boxer is 'tidied up' around the muzzle area.

LEFT: Stray hairs are trimmed from the Boxer's tail in order to present a clean outline.

FACING PAGE: In the Ring: Keep your eye on the judge at all times, so that you can ensure your Boxer is looking his best when he is being assessed.

Johnson

entered in the correct class. If he is not, contact the secretary. Be sure to exercise your dog well before you are due in the ring and clean up afterwards.

As the class before yours goes in, give your Boxer a last-minute groom, put on his show lead and get to the ring so that you are ready when the steward calls your class. Stand where the steward asks you to, and set your dog up as best you can. Watch the old hands and how they approach the job, talk to your dog all the time and do your best to put him at his ease.

When the judge goes over your Boxer, you may be asked the dog's age, in which case answer the question. It is bad form to engage a judge in conversation. Speak when spoken to is the golden rule. Be sure to follow the judge's requests. If you are asked for a triangle in movement, try to master a triangle – no other geometric variation.

Once the class has been seen, be sure to have your dog standing and looking his best. Try to keep one eye on your dog, and one on the judge. Your dog may fidget and move a leg, so it is important that you notice this before the judge does. If you are lucky enough to be pulled out, stand where the judge or steward asks you to. You may be required to move again before the final placings are made. If you receive a prize-card, a polite thank you to the steward is basic good manners. Congratulating those placed above you always creates a good impression, and feel free to shake their hands.

In the event of being fortunate enough to win your class, you are then classed as an 'unbeaten dog' and, unless you are entered in any subsequent classes, you will be needed to challenge for Best Dog, Best Bitch or Best of Breed. Be sure to watch the judging so that you do not delay this final award. Latecomers do not endear themselves to either judges or stewards. If you should win Best of Breed, you owe it to your breed to stay for the Best in Show or Group competition. Check with the show manager at what time this is likely to take place, and be there on time.

Whether you win or lose, always remember that the Boxer you are taking home with you after the show is exactly the same dog you brought with you that morning. Make sure you both enjoy the day – after all, show-going is a hobby!

Chapter Six

BREEDING BOXERS

MAKING AN INFORMED DECISION

When your Boxer has reached adulthood, there may come a time when you think it would be a good idea to get involved with breeding. This could be occasioned, in the case of a bitch, by someone assuring you that "a litter would do her good" – which is, incidentally, rubbish – or simply by wanting to have a descendant of your much-loved Boxer. My immediate advice is – Don't go ahead! Breeding dogs in general, and Boxers in particular, is a hobby which should not be embarked upon on a whim. It requires knowledge of the breed and breeding, it demands total dedication and a lot of hard work, and it also requires sound financial backing. This is all provided you have a good enough animal to breed from in the first place.

In the case of a male dog, you may think that it should be his right to sample the pleasures of the flesh just once. But you are wrong. To begin with, a stud dog is not just a male dog with two testicles. A stud dog is a dog who is bred from sound breeding stock, who has been bred to breed on. He should possess great virtues with regard to the Breed Standard, and only minimal faults.

You may be approached by someone with a pet Boxer bitch who is interested in mating their bitch to your dog, but it is far kinder to deny your dog any studs at all, than to let him serve a bitch just once. This can be guaranteed to build up mental frustration, and the lack of regular stud work may prompt him to acquire quite anti-social habits. In truth, unless your Boxer dog has proved a great winner in the show ring, it will be unlikely that even occasional stud work will come his way, so, in this case, the old adage of "what you've never had, you will never miss" really does apply.

Your Boxer may be a bitch, and many owners of pet bitches tend to breed them for all the wrong reasons. The most common is, as mentioned earlier, that having a litter would be good for her. In fact, many Boxer bitches lead perfectly normal, happy, healthy lives, never having had puppies. If you feel you would like to sustain family continuity after your bitch has passed on, it would be a lot more sensible to return to the breeder and possibly acquire a relative, such as a niece, as it is highly likely that the breeder will always have related stock available.

Apart from the great demands of whelping and rearing a litter, there is the question of the puppies' future. It is highly unlikely that you, as a pet owner, will have a substantial waiting list of would-be puppy buyers, and remember that your bitch could have up to ten puppies in her litter. That means that there will be the appropriate number of good, responsible, loving homes to be found. You may think that advertising the pups when they are eight weeks old will bring crowds to your

A brood bitch should be a fine representative of the breed, with a sound, trustworthy temperament.

The stud dog should complement your bitch in terms of her pedigree and her physical characteristics.

Tail docking is becoming an increasingly controversial issue, and you will have to decide whether you want your puppies' tails to be docked or left in their natural state.

The food ration should only be increased in the last few weeks of pregnancy. It is important that the bitch is in a fit, supple condition in preparation for whelping.

door, but it is not that simple. Most people who are looking for a puppy will do just as you did, and approach one of the reputable breeders. What chance does that give you? It is folly to even consider mating your bitch unless you are sure of several good homes that are lined up well in advance.

Can you imagine the mess made by a litter of active baby Boxer puppies, not to mention the cost of rearing them properly? Have you thought of the facilities you will need for whelping and rearing a litter? You must have enough space to install a whelping box and puppy run, and that area must be warm, draught-proof, and quiet. Breeding a litter will mean that someone has to be at home, virtually twenty-four hours a day, for two months. Are you prepared to disrupt your routine to that extent?

These are just some of the points which you must consider very seriously before you think about mating your Boxer bitch. Once you have thought the whole thing through, you have contacted friends and members of your family who have expressed a genuine desire to have one of your bitch's puppies, and you are still determined to breed a litter, the hard work begins in earnest.

HEREDITARY CONSIDERATIONS
As the Boxer is your chosen breed, you should have researched the breed sufficiently to know that it is subject, in some cases, to hereditary conditions, which you would not want to perpetuate. Overall the Boxer is a healthy breed, but breeders do not ignore the fact that these hereditary problems can and do crop up from time to time, and all are anxious to avoid them. These include progressive axonopathy, hip dysplasia and heart conditions (see Chapter Seven: Health Care).

THE STUD DOG
When you have established that your bitch is suitable to use for breeding, you then have to choose a stud dog. It is a good idea to attend a few Boxer shows, if you do not do so regularly, and look at the dogs in the ring – and also the bitches. Some of the dogs will appeal to you more than others, and if you have done your homework and studied the breed, this should in theory be because they are better Boxers. Make a note of the dogs which appeal to you and find out who their sire is. You may discover that you have chosen several dogs who share the same sire. That is good, as it means that you are developing your 'eye'.

When you have found a dog who has produced several offspring you admire, make a point of going to see the dog himself, if you are not already familiar with him. Be open with his owner and tell him that you are contemplating breeding a litter. Show him your bitch's pedigree and ask for comments. By studying the pedigree of both your bitch and the prospective stud dog, you will be able to see if there are any similarities. It is important that you find out as much as you can about any dogs which are common to both pedigrees.

Line-breeding is the method of breeding by which related dogs are bred together, in an attempt to maintain the same type. But it is vital that you understand that line-breeding must be carried out for the right reasons, otherwise it can do more harm than good. For example, let us suppose that you are comparing the pedigrees of your bitch and prospective stud dog and discover that they both share the same grandsire. He was a well-known Champion dog who produced many excellent puppies, and stamped his type. The chances are, should you go ahead with this mating, that at least some of the puppies will bear a resemblance to their common great-grandsire.

However, on the other hand, you may discover that the only common dog in the pedigrees is an unshown bitch who appears as grand-dam to your bitch, and great-grand-dam to the dog. It could be that the bitch in question had produced good stock by being mated to superior, unrelated dogs, to improve on a major fault she carried. Perhaps she had a very poor mouth which was badly wry and too much undershot. Although this fault may not have manifested itself either in the pedigree of your bitch, or in the pedigree of her suitor, when you mate the two together you stand a strong chance of producing puppies which may have this mouth fault, if to a lesser degree. In order to line-breed successfully, you must be confident that you are only 'doubling up' on virtues, and not on serious faults.

This is where talking to the older and more experienced breeders can be of great help, because they will probably have known many of the dogs and bitches way back in your bitch's pedigree, and will be able to tell you what they were like. It is helpful to get as much of this kind of information as possible beforehand, to build up a visual picture of your bitch's ancestry.

Eventually you will have decided upon your chosen stud dog, and his owner will obviously want to see your bitch before committing himself. Believe it or not, most breeders and stud dog owners are not just interested in the stud fees. The stud dog owner may well take one look at your bitch and tell you that the pair are not compatible. Perhaps she may be a little short on the leg, and your chosen stud dog tends to throw short rather than tall. In this case, most stud dog owners will suggest an alternative sire, rather than risk producing sub-standard puppies which would be a poor reflection on their stud dog.

Discuss the stud fee and any special arrangements. If the stud dog owner likes the look of your bitch and thinks the mating could produce something good, he may offer to take a puppy rather than charging you a stud fee. In fact, if such an offer is made, that is a good sign that the litter you have planned should be of high quality. If you make this sort of arrangement, make sure that the details are put down in writing. You must be clear in your own mind as to what the stud dog owner is entitled to take from the litter. On the subject of stud fees, please remember that if you elect to pay a fee, you are paying for the stud service itself, not for puppies. Customarily, should your bitch fail to conceive, most stud dog owners will offer you a return service free of charge. But that is neither their obligation nor your right.

BREEDING TERMS

It is worth saying a few words about breeding terms, as these can often cause great disharmony. Sometimes a breeder will sell a bitch into a pet home, charging a reduced price for the bitch and planning to take one or more puppies from a litter which the buyer has undertaken to breed. At first this might seem like an attractive arrangement, as the buyer has to pay far less for his initial purchase. Beware! Breeding terms can be disastrous and have been known to end up in a court of law!

I would advise that you only become involved in breeding terms as a last resort. The whole business is fraught with problems. Your bitch may be in season and her breeder wants you to mate her. It may not be convenient for you as you are planning a family holiday, but the breeder will not wait a further six months for his puppy. You may have agreed to give the breeder first and third pick from the litter,

ABOVE: The bitch will care for all the puppies' needs in the first couple of weeks, feeding them and cleaning them.

RIGHT: A contented litter will make little noise in the early stages. They will alternate periods of feeding with periods of sleep.

ABOVE:
Weaning starts
when the puppies
are three to four
weeks old,
depending on
their physical
development.

LEFT: Feeding
from communal
dishes increases
the puppies'
determination to
get to the food.
Watch out for
any smaller or
weaker puppies,
who might not be
getting their fair
share.

yet your bitch only has three puppies, leaving you with just one. The breeder may wish to have the bitch in his ownership for the litter so that he can register them with his kennel name, and be officially recorded as the breeder of the litter. Is this acceptable to you? Breeding terms are to be avoided, and if you must get involved in such an arrangement, again be sure to have everything watertight in a written agreement.

AN AFFIX
You will have noted that your bitch's Kennel Club registered name has two parts – the kennel name (or affix) and her given name. In human terms, a surname, followed by a Christian name. If her breeder's kennel name is 'Boxerlands', your bitch may be called 'Boxerlands Scarlet Samba'. When you come to breed a litter, you may wish to register your own affix so that all your puppies will carry your own unique 'family name'. You will need to complete a special form from the Kennel Club, applying for an affix, and will probably have to submit several choices in order of preference.

People choose their affixes through various methods – house names, a combination of the owners' names, or something relating to their original bitch. In the case of your Scarlet Samba, you might think that 'Scaramba' would be appropriate, considering her name. The choice is unlimited and deciding on an affix can be fun, but remember that your puppies' names will have a maximum number of 24 letters including the affix, so make it short rather than long.

THE MATING
You have chosen your stud dog, the owner has approved your bitch, and you have advised when your bitch is due in season. Depending on when she first came in season, the second or third season is ideal for a first litter but it is inadvisable to breed from a Boxer bitch before she is eighteen months old.

When she starts her season, a bright discharge is noticeable; this is when you should first notify the stud dog owner. Some stud dog owners insist on a vet taking a vaginal swab to ensure there is no infection. This should be done as soon as your bitch comes in season. Most Boxer bitches are mated around the eleventh day of their season, but no two are alike and some need to be mated very early, others much later. The best way of telling whether is bitch is ready is the stud dog's reaction to her. A good yardstick for ascertaining the bitch's readiness is when her bright red discharge begins to pale. You will at this time probably find that when you tickle her at the side of her tail, she will flick it to one side. This is a very promising sign of her readiness to accept a dog. As soon as this occurs, telephone the stud dog owner and make arrangements for the visit.

The chances are that you will be using a dog who is owned by someone who is experienced in stud work, so simply do as the owner asks. It is not a good idea, if you are a typical 'pet' owner, to become involved with the actual mating. Many such owners tend to become rather emotional when their precious bitch lets out so much as a little squeak (as they invariably do) when the dog penetrates, and when trying to effect a mating between two substantial Boxers, the last thing the owner of the dog needs is an hysterical owner confusing the issue!

Most stud dog owners will suggest that you bring the bitch in, on the lead, to be introduced to the dog – who will also be on a lead at this stage. (For the actual mating the bitch should wear a strong leather collar as she will need to be held.) They will flirt, the dog will sniff the bitch and if she is ready, he will make no secret of the fact that he is raring to go. The owner will probably suggest that you go off for a cup of coffee at this juncture, and leave it to the experts. That is sound advice. There will probably be at least two experienced people at hand to effect the mating, and practice really does make perfect.

If your bitch is ready, and the dog is keen, after the initial flirtation the dog will mount the bitch and eventually penetrate her. During these proceedings, your bitch will have been held by her collar to avoid her snapping at the dog, a perfectly normal reaction but one which can sometimes cause injury to the intrepid male. Once he has penetrated, the dog will swell up inside the bitch, effecting a 'tie', which can last for anything up to an hour. Once tied, the dog will be turned in such a way that the dog and bitch will be standing, tail-to-tail, the dog still inside the bitch.

When they are tied, you will probably be invited to see your bitch, if only to reassure you that she has been mated to the right dog! When the tie breaks, your bitch will be given a drink of water and she should then be put in the car to rest.

Sort out the paperwork with the stud dog owner, who will give you a copy of the dog's pedigree, a signed form for the Kennel Club registration of the puppies, certifying that the mating took place, and any 'puppy back' arrangements should be committed to print. If you are breeding a litter with no real plans for enlarging your Boxer family yourself, letting the sire's owner take a puppy or two at least means that there are fewer good homes for you to find.

PREPARING FOR THE WHELPING

Far too many amateur breeders make the fatal mistake of cramming their bitch with every additive on the market during pregnancy – if only they knew what harm they were doing! As long as your bitch is enjoying a fully balanced diet, she should have nothing more than a slightly increased food intake during the last few weeks of the usual 63-day gestation period. As she gets bigger, the bitch will appreciate having a food ration divided into two or three small meals a day. Some breeders still swear by giving their in-whelp bitches raspberry-leaf tablets to ease the whelping. This is a wholly natural product and can do no harm, but again consult with your breeder and read the label!

Your bitch should have been wormed prior to mating, and it is advisable to worm her again about five weeks after the mating – but no later. For years, and before the advent of all the complete feeding regimes, breeders gave hefty doses of calcium to in-whelp bitches, but modern thinking suggests that this can contribute to eclampsia. This is a condition caused by lack of calcium in the blood, and nowadays it is more usual to administer calcium only post-whelping.

You need to establish exactly where your bitch is to whelp, and, ideally, you should invest in a large whelping box, if possible with a collapsible puppy-run made up of mesh panels. This can be placed around the box when the puppies are beginning to walk. Provided your whelping area is at room temperature, you should not need any further heating, but if you are using an outside utility area, it may be necessary to install an infra-red lamp over the whelping box – always ensuring that the lamp is not too low.

If you are getting a whelping box, be sure to find one that has 'pig rails' around all four sides, so there is no danger that a puppy may be suffocated underneath a

ABOVE: In no time, the puppies start to emerge as individuals in their own right.

LEFT: Clean, fresh water should be available to the litter.

ABOVE: Socialisation should begin while the puppies are still with the breeder. This pup is meeting the family cat for the first time.

BELOW: Rest is essential for growing puppies. The pups derive warmth and comfort from sleeping with each other.

careless Mum. You need to build up a stock of newspapers, and also buy at least three pieces of the marvellous polyester-fur type blankets which are now easily available. These allow fluids to drain through to newspapers below, but remain dry on the surface. They are one of the greatest inventions for dog breeders; they should be the same size as your whelping box's floor area. You will need three pieces because they will need washing constantly and you will find that at any one time you will have one in the box and one in the wash!

On the wall above the whelping box pin a card upon which should be written two very important telephone numbers – your veterinarian and your bitch's breeder. This is in case of emergencies only, but if you should have a problem and panic, you need to know exactly where these numbers are.

During the eighth week of pregnancy you should introduce your bitch to the whelping quarters. If she is prepared to sleep in the whelping box, let her do so. As her due date approaches she will be glad to seek the solace of her quiet, comfortable retreat. Near the 63rd day of pregnancy, you will notice your bitch becoming restless, she will probably go off her food, and if you take her temperature you will find that it has dropped to around 97 degrees Fahrenheit (35 degrees Centigrade). When whelping is imminent, the bitch will begin to pant. At this stage she should be put in the whelping box, and any intruders such as children or other pets should be prevented from distracting her. She will now be happy to stay in her whelping box and will probably start scratching furiously.

THE WHELPING

As labour progresses, your bitch will begin her contractions and eventually you may notice a balloon-like bag appearing through her vulva. Do not panic. This is the membrane containing her first puppy. Puppies are normally born head-first, but sometimes come through a breech-birth. In the event of a breech, the birth may not be as easy as if head-first, so you should be ready to help. Using a towel, hold the puppy's rear and, taking a firm but gentle grip, pull slowly when she bears down. Do not tug or be rough as you may damage the puppy.

Once the puppy is born, remove the membrane and place the puppy at the bitch's head so that she can sever the umbilical cord and eat the afterbirth. Novice breeders may be appalled at this apparently unsavoury practice, but it is quite natural as consuming the afterbirth helps promote antibodies in the milk. If your bitch has any problem biting the umbilical cord, you should have a pair of sterilised scissors to hand, and cut the cord a few inches away from the puppy.

Your bitch will now be licking her puppy furiously, drying it, and pushing life into it. You may think she is being rather rough with the puppy, but do not worry, puppies are quite hardy and 'mother knows best'. Once she has cleaned up the pup and it seems normal, try to put it on to a teat and encourage it to suckle. Most puppies do so quite naturally.

Boxer bitches will vary as to how long they go between producing puppies. Some will have them like shelling peas; others will go for hours between puppies. If three hours have elapsed and there are no signs of any further births, contact your vet, as your bitch may need an inducing injection. It is possible that your bitch might experience some difficulty in passing her puppies. If she seems unduly distressed, you should again call out your vet as a caesarean section may be called for, in which case you will need to get her to the surgery promptly. 'Caesars' are not that common in Boxers, but they are sometimes necessary.

At the end of a normal whelping, your bitch should be happy with her babies, and will appear tired but contented. This is the time to call your vet and get him to check your bitch over. He should confirm that all is well and mother and babies are fine. Once all your puppies are delivered and suckling, leave your bitch in what is guaranteed to be a horribly messy whelping box for about half an hour, and then encourage her to leave her family and go outside to relieve herself.

While she is away, put the puppies on a blanket in a cardboard box and remove the newspapers, which will be covered in a mixture of green discharge and blood. Dry out the whelping box, put down a layer of clean newspapers and a clean piece of the fleecy bedding you have to hand. Put the puppies back into the box and call mother back in. She will not need asking a second time! She may also be grateful for a drink of water with some glucose in it at this stage.

POST-WHELPING

Now to one of the less pleasant aspects of breeding a litter of Boxer puppies. Your bitch may have had one or more white puppies. Before the whelping, you should have made up your mind as to what you intend doing with such puppies. Unless they are colour-patched (which indicates a reduced risk of deafness) and you have a definite, guaranteed home waiting for a white puppy, the kindest thing is to have them humanely destroyed when your vet comes to give the bitch a check-over. The puppies should also be checked for cleft palates or any other major deformity which may call for euthanasia.

Constantly check your bitch's teats for any small lumps which may herald the onset of mastitis. If you find lumps, wash the teats with warm water and ask your vet to visit, as a course of antibiotics may be necessary. Your bitch should be eating small meals often, and do not be keen to overdo the additives. Seek advice from your bitch's breeder, and always follow the manufacturers' instructions.

When the puppies are a few days old, they will need to have their dew-claws removed. Tails must be docked at this stage, if this is what you have decided to do. This is a sensitive issue, as in Britain many vets refuse to dock tails. Before your bitch was mated, you should have confirmed your vet's policy on tails.

WARNING SIGNS

Your bitch will continue to discharge a heavy, bloody fluid for a few days after whelping. This is quite natural. There may be a slight discharge for as long as eight weeks after whelping. If the discharge becomes bright red in colour, call in your vet as it could signal the start of a womb infection.

Eclampsia has been mentioned before, and if the bitch's system is drained of calcium, she could become unsteady on her legs, her eyes may appear glazed, and she may act strangely with her puppies, perhaps trying to 'bury' them. Any such symptoms should be dealt with immediately by your vet.

WEANING

Weaning can start in earnest at about three-to-four weeks of age, and at this stage it is a good idea to ask your vet's advice regarding worming both your bitch and her puppies. All puppies will have tiny roundworms, and they need eliminating as soon as possible.

Provide safe toys for the puppies to play with. These 'games' help the puppies' mental and physical development.

RIGHT: The best way to assess a puppy is to stand him on the table.

BELOW: This Boxer puppy is now ready to take his place in the world with his new owners.

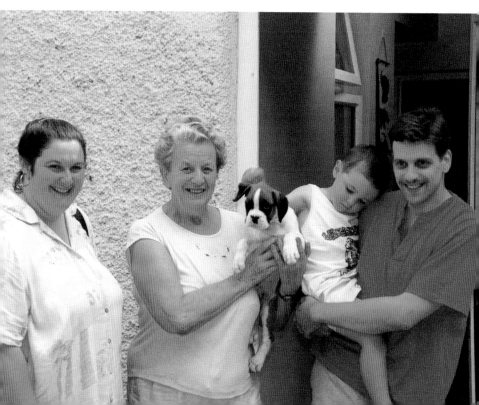

No two breeders will wean in exactly the same way, so the chances are that you will adopt a similar method to that used by your own bitch's breeder. Some breeders prefer to wean their puppies on to raw red meat, while others will start them off immediately with a proprietary puppy food. Either way, the puppies' first taste of solid food can be given on your finger. The pups will soon become interested in 'real' food, and within a short time they will happily eat from a bowl.

Most breeders tend to give two meat meals and two milk-based meals per day to baby puppies. Some breeders prefer to feed puppies individually, ensuring that they all get their fair share. Others work on the theory that one large food bowl stimulates healthy competition and healthy appetites, but there is the danger that less forward puppies will be pushed into the background and not get their just deserts. Within reason, puppies up to eight weeks should be allowed to eat as much as they want. Happily, Boxers tend to be 'good doers' and are seldom picky with their food.

THE GROWING PUPPIES

You will to need keep a close eye on your puppies' nails as they grow at an alarming rate. These nails may be small, but they can cause great pain to the bitch when the puppies are suckling, unless they are trimmed regularly. Human nail-clippers can be used for this task, which should be carried out at least once a week. Bitches are reluctant to let their puppies feed if they know they are likely to be ripped to shreds!

When puppies are up and walking, you should make sure that the whelping box is enclosed with a puppy pen. This will ensure that curious puppies do not stray. It is always beneficial if the puppy run can be somewhere central to the household, as puppies need to get used to everyday noises from an early age. The best adjusted puppies are those who have been reared in busy surroundings, rather than in an isolated kennel.

Your Boxer bitch will soon let you know when she is ready to leave her puppies. Her milk supply will diminish, and she will be reluctant to lie with her puppies for any length of time. Most bitches are quite happy to leave their family by about five weeks of age, and move back into the household proper.

When your puppies are weaned, it is a good idea to let visitors to your home handle them, as this helps to socialise them, but be sure to disinfect strangers' hands, as disease may be easily transmitted.

By the time the litter is eight weeks old, the puppies should be ready to go to their new homes. You will have given them all the love and attention in the world, and parting with them is not going to be easy. All you can do for them now is ensure that they are going to owners who will look after them as well as you have. In the coming months, you will be thrilled to receive photographs of the puppies as they grow up, with news of their development and adolescence. From time to time, they will drop by with their owners, and you will derive great joy from your extended Boxer family.

Chapter Seven

HEALTH CARE

The Boxer is a naturally hardy breed and relatively maintenance-free. However, each week, when you are giving him his regular grooming session, you should check his ears, eyes, teeth and coat. If your Boxer appears to be off-colour or off his food give him twenty-fours hours and if there is no noticeable improvement contact your vet. Symptoms which are spotted early can often prevent a condition from becoming more serious.

COMMON AILMENTS

ANAL GLANDS: The only other area which may need watching is the anal glands. These are two glands situated at either side of the anus. Sometimes, and for no apparent reason, they can become impacted. The indication of this happening could be your Boxer dragging himself along on his bottom, a barely apparent swelling in this area, or the occasional detection of a foul smell. Expressing the glands is simple, taking just seconds, an experienced hand and a goodly supply of tissues, but it is best left to the vet. Inexperienced attempts could cause mild injury.

BLOAT: Bloat is a condition which results from fermenting foods releasing gas into the stomach, sometimes causing the stomach to twist. It is a serious condition, and it must be dealt with instantly by your vet as it can prove fatal. There are various theories as to the cause of bloat, but none are scientifically proven. As a preventative, it is advisable to feed two small meals rather than one large meal if a complete diet is used, and exercise should be restricted for a few hours after a meal.

BURNS: Burns and scalds should be dealt with immediately. Apply cold water to the affected area to ease the pain, then take your dog to the vet as soon as possible.

CUTS AND WOUNDS: Inevitably, at some stage of your Boxer's life, he will suffer a minor cut or a wound of some sort. In the case of small cuts and gashes, cleaning with a mild disinfectant and treating with an antiseptic ointment should be all that is necessary. Larger wounds may need stitching by your veterinarian, and deep wounds may be subject to infection, requiring a course of antibiotics. Cut pads can be difficult to deal with, for obvious reasons, but if the cut is small, cleaning as detailed above, can soon be followed by treating with a proprietary brand of 'new skin' solution, which is painted on and forms a protective layer, thus speeding the healing process.

FACING PAGE: Keep a regular check on your Boxer's overall condition, and this should ensure that you spot any health problems before they become serious. Photo: Diane Pearce.

RIGHT: The elderly Boxer deserves special consideration to ensure his continued well-being.

BELOW: The Boxer will slow up as he gets older, but he can still enjoy a good quality of life.

CYSTS: Boxers are prone to developing small cysts in middle age and beyond. Most remain small and benign, and may never require treatment. However, if a cyst seems to be growing rapidly, veterinary advice should be sought. Interdigital cysts (between the toes) can often be painful, and these may require surgery.

HEAT STROKE: Most Boxers love the sun, but too much sun-bathing can bring on heat stroke. If your Boxer is adversely affected, he will be shaky on his legs and his temperature will be unduly high. Try to reduce the temperature by applying ice-packs (large packs of frozen peas from your freezer, wrapped in a towel, are ideal in an emergency), and keep the dog in a cool, shady place.

Never leave your Boxer in a car, even on a moderately warm day, as a parked car will serve as an oven. Dogs die in hot cars regularly, so make sure you never take the risk.

POISONING: Boxers are curious, and your dog may be tempted to chew at something in your garden which may, unknown to you, present a potential danger. If you notice that your Boxer is a little shaky on his legs, glassy-eyed, and rather disorientated, there is a chance that he has taken in a noxious substance. The best course of action is to pour cooking salt down the dog's throat, followed by a little water which will make him vomit. Then ask your vet to check the dog over.

STINGS: Boxers are fascinated by bees, wasps and other buzzing insects. Often their curiosity is harmless, but occasionally a sting will result. If this is external, treat the area with an antiseptic solution, and then apply a paste of bicarbonate of soda and water. If the sting is in the mouth, apply ice-cubes to the affected area and consult your vet immediately.

STOMACH UPSETS: Routinely you should get into the habit of checking your Boxer's motions when you clean up after him. They should always be firm and free from worms. If they are loose, your Boxer probably has an upset stomach. The best course of action is to starve your dog for twenty-four hours making sure that fresh drinking water is readily available. When you resume feeding, offer plain food such as fish or cooked chicken and rice. If your Boxer still has diarrhoea, consult the vet.

INHERITED CONDITIONS

PROGRESSIVE AXONOPATHY: After the Second World War, large and strong Boxer kennels emerged on both sides of the Atlantic, many of them sharing common foundation stock. To this day, imports continue to arrive in the UK at a steady pace, although not in such volume as was seen in the 1980s. The reason for this sudden influx was not so much to facilitate gradual improvement of the breed; it was done out of necessity and desperation. The reason can be summed up in two letters – PA. To this day, these two letters send shivers down the spines of British Boxer breeders.

In the late 1970s several Boxer breeders in the UK reported cases of Boxer puppies, sometimes as old as six months, going off their back legs and gradually becoming paralysed. The condition was incurable, and the agony of watching a much-loved companion going through such agony was more than some owners could bear. At first it was thought that the instances reported were simply isolated cases, but as more and more information was gathered, it became apparent that Progressive Axonopathy was a debilitating disease which affected the nervous system. Furthermore, it seemed to be specific to the Boxer breed and, worst of all, it was of an hereditary nature.

Various theories were put forward as to how this genetic problem appeared, and through much sterling work carried out by Dr Ian Griffiths and Dr Bruce Cattanach, who is not only a geneticist but a successful Boxer breeder as well, it was determined that the PA gene was a simple recessive. To this day, there is no certainty as to how or why it should appear. In practical terms, this meant that a Boxer could be clinically normal and healthy, yet still carry the gene. When two carriers were unwittingly bred together, disaster could strike and they could produce puppies which were affected by PA.

One of the most heartbreaking aspects of this dreadful disease is the fact that it does not become apparent until the puppy may be reaching puberty. Imagine the distress when pet owners, having brought home, house-trained, schooled and lavished love and affection on their new puppy, suddenly find it off its legs with only one tragic solution. Despite the initial turmoil within the breed, Boxer breeders and the Boxer Breed Council (set up from all the various regional and national breed clubs) took the bull by the horns and determined to do their level best to save the breed and eradicate PA. Supervised test matings were carried out between carriers and 'unknowns' in an attempt to clear dogs, and gradually some light could be seen at the end of the tunnel.

Some breeders had no alternative but to stand back and write off what was, in many cases, a lifetime's work. Top winning dogs were castrated and given away to pet homes, hitherto valuable brood bitches were spayed, and some breeders had to simply start from scratch with newly-acquired breeding stock, a lot of which was imported from other countries where PA was unheard of. It says much for the resilience of the British Boxer breeders that the breed is now very much on top of the PA situation and cases are seldom seen, though anyone even contemplating breeding a litter of Boxer puppies must do their utmost to research the pedigrees of the prospective parents and consult with experts in the field of PA beforehand.

So how do you avoid producing a PA puppy? Firstly, it is to be hoped that your bitch has been produced from clear stock, but this should be confirmed by the breeder. You should then get hold of an information leaflet about the disease, along with a list of cleared and carrier dogs, which can be obtained through your local Boxer club. It is essential to know that your bitch is from clear lines. Check her pedigree thoroughly against the list, and make sure that there are no carrier dogs in her pedigree. If the pedigree seems clear, that is the first hurdle ovecome.

HEART CONDITIONS: Some Boxer lines seem to be affected with heart problems. This may mean nothing more than a slight murmur which will not affect a Boxer's quality of life at all; others may be more serious.

If you are planning to breed from your Boxer bitch, you should do your utmost to ensure that she is physically fit enough for the whelping, and heart testing should be considered essential. Testing sessions are arranged at many Boxer shows, but your vet can also carry out the simple test.

HIP DYSPLASIA: Hip Dysplasia is another hereditary condition which affects some Boxers to a minor degree. Ascertaining the level of dysplasia, if it exists, involves X-raying a dog under general anaesthetic, and the resulting X-rays are then sent to a professional body which scores them against the norm for the breed.

THE VETERAN BOXER

CARING FOR THE OLDER DOG

As your Boxer enters the last few years of life, he will find difficulty in doing much of what was taken for granted when in his prime. He will generally slow down, and some of his vital organs may let him down. Old dogs – like people – become arthritic. It is therefore essential that your ageing Boxer has a bed which is firm yet soft, low to the ground, and completely draught-free. There are several types of bed available which are manufactured especially for the elderly dog. Exercise should be reduced if your dog has become arthritic.

As time goes by, your Boxer may require medication to help with a condition which has developed with old age. In this case, veterinary advice should always be followed. With regard to feeding, your Boxer's meals can be reduced slightly in quantity, but increase the frequency of meals. A high consumption of fluids may signal the onset of ailing kidneys.

Caring for the veteran Boxer requires patience and understanding; at all times, the quality of life should be uppermost in your mind. A change of lifestyle may be called for, but, with minor adjustments, many Boxers enjoy their pensioner years.

THE FINAL PARTING

Much as it pains us, dogs do not live nearly as long as we would like them to. Boxers, on average, live for around twelve years or so. Some make much older bones; others regretfully die younger.

It is every dog owner's hope that their pal will, when the time has come, die peacefully in his sleep, thus relieving his owner of the terrible burden of having to make a heart-rending decision.

Should your Boxer become old and infirm, what should be uppermost in your mind is his quality of life. Too many owners put off making 'that' decision, not out of concern for the dog, but to spare their own feelings, which is wrong. Your Boxer will have led a happy, active life. If he becomes incontinent, or crippled with arthritis, he will lose his pride and his independence. When this happens, you must think long and hard if it really is the kindest thing to drag out a life which is becoming miserable.

Your Boxer will have given you one hundred per cent loyalty throughout his life. You owe it to him to do the same, and much as it might hurt you, there may come a time when the kindest thing for your Boxer is for you to ensure that he leaves this world with dignity.

His passing will leave a great void in your life, and you may feel you can never give your heart to another Boxer. But time heals, and you will gradually remember all the good times you spent together, all the joy he brought to you, and the thrill you felt when you first saw the face of that mischievous little puppy. And that is when it all starts again!